The Scottish

HOGMANAY!

Handbook

The Scottish
HOGMANAY!
Handbook

The Complete Guide to
Celebrating New Year in true
Scottish Style

Gordon Fraser

BroadSword Books

The Scottish Hogmanay Handbook

First published in Great Britain in MCMXCVIII by BroadSword Books, PO Box 10249, AB11 7YP

Typeset in 12 pt Century Schoolbook

CONTENTS

INTRODUCTION

A Highland Fling with a difference...

Hogmanay, or New Year's Eve in Scotland, what could be better? The fun, the laughter and all the old traditions. From the bustling crowds, beneath Edinburgh Castle, on Princes Street to the smallest Highland croft there are Hogmanay celebrations going on. But what exactly is Hogmanay and just what are the traditions? A time of the year shrouded in superstition Hogmanay is more than simply a big party – it is a time for change, a time when good or bad luck hangs in the balance. So how do you make sure you keep the bad luck away for the next year and the good luck coming your way? And how do you hold a real Scottish Hogmanay celebration that combines all the great traditions with having one of the best parties possible?

Renowned for their New Year's Eve shenanigans, the Scots have much good cheer to offer everyone through their traditional parties. And the fact-filled Scottish Hogmanay! Handbook is here to help provide you with all the help you should need to have a great New Year's Eve party - as well as giving you lots of other useful information and tips to guide you through this marvellous New Year tradition.

This is not to say, however, that celebrating New Year is purely a Scottish event, far from it.

Recognising the coming of New Year is the oldest and most ancient of all holidays, first being observed by the ancient Babylonians some four thousand years ago! Nor has New Year always been marked on the same date. For many, many years the end of March, due to the coming of Spring, was seen by our ancestors, quite logically, as the beginning of the year when they began crop planting. The 1st January date we now all know so well has no astronomical or agricultural significance being purely arbitrary and, as a result, has really only been celebrated in Scotland since 1600.

Scotland though, has made the celebration of New Year something of its own, blending its own traditions and fun-filled spirit into the event we now know as Hogmanay. True, Hogmanay parties can have something of a reputation for being high-spirited due to the fact that in bygone days it was one of only a few days each year when people were allowed off from work to have a party and really enjoy themselves. But regardless of how enthusiastic our modern Hogmanay celebrations get, they pale in comparison to those of our ancient ancestors.

So while Hogmanay has its traditions in the worker's day off it is still very much a family occasion and lots of fun for the younger members of the family too, with singing, dancing and party games – not to mention the added thrill for the youngsters of staying up late to see in the new year. Above all the coming of the New Year is a chance to socialise, throw a big Hogmanay party, renew old friendships and have a lot of fun – wherever you are and whatever your nationality.

This book has, therefore, been written for both Scots and foreign visitors so includes, where possible, as much explanation, clarification and background information on all the various topics raised as well as coming with a useful glossary of words at the end. This means that, for some native readers, there are certain passages which will, no doubt, be somewhat familiar but we're sure that there's plenty of other, more unusual, information to help you get the most out of your Hogmanay. Have fun!

CHAPTER ONE

Happy Hogmanay!

● ●

The Origins of 'Hogmanay'

After Christmas, Hogmanay and the coming of the New Year has to be one of the best times of the year.

In Scotland, and for Scots in general wherever they are, there is a particular fondness for Hogmanay. It is a time when they think of their nation, remember its traditions and celebrate the future. Hogmanay means, amongst many other things, swinging ceilidhs, drinking the water of life (or whisky), observing the old customs and belting out Auld Lang Syne with your proudest voice.

The origins of the word 'Hogmanay' - the name given by Scots to the 31 December is wrapped in some confusion. Some believe the word to be derived from the old northern French dialect word 'hogu-inan,' meaning 'last day of the year' and was a song sung by children as they 'guised' or went from door to door collecting gifts. Others prefer to believe that it means 'hug-me-now' and began when social kissing in public was much more common. Indeed Scotland's finest poet Robert Burns commented that much kissing occurred "on the happy nights of hog-ma-nay [where] the kissing trade is extremely brisk, particularly in Auld Reekie (Edinburgh); then the lasses (girls) must kiss with all the stranger lads they meet, while phrases not unlike 'John, come kiss me now' or 'John, come hug me now' are frequently heard."

Another explanation links the word to the old custom of 'first footing', which requires the first visitor of the New Year to bring a present with them, this, some say indicates its origin to the old French word 'aguillan-neuf' – an occasion for distributing gifts. This might well be so considering how few 'free' days there were to give gifts. Indeed, for many years, Hogmanay was the only holiday in Scotland which many servants and workers had throughout winter and was more associated with the giving of gifts than Christmas - which for many was just another religious day of work.

From whatever source you care to choose, Hogmanay is a very important time of the year, to cast out the old, evil spirits and begin afresh. It should always mean a time of good cheer, happiness and of hope for the good times ahead!

HOGMANAY IN SCOTLAND

Hogmanay is celebrated all over Scotland, from the smallest croft in the Highlands to the major street parties of the larger cities. Everywhere you go you'll find events being organised, with traditional dancing, music, party games, talk, fun and laughter and, of course, a fair amount of 'water of life' or whisky being drunk.

It is, however, very much a family affair with a great deal of socialising by all the generations from grand-parents to grandchildren. In days gone by there were also 'guisers', usually children, who would dress up and go from house to house collecting small gifts of food and, although this is no longer generally done, firework displays, street carnivals, ships (and cars) sounding their horns plus bell ringing ensures that Hogmanay does not pass un-noticed in Scotland.

Edinburgh

If you want to be part of the biggest Hogmanay street party in the world then the celebration on Edinburgh's main thoroughfare, Princes Street, is the place to be. Wide and with a great view of Edinburgh Castle this street has become the focal point for around two hundred thousand revellers. With bands playing, carnivals, pipe-bands, fun-fares, parades, a torchlight procession as well as thousands of people dancing – not to mention a lot of cheer, every year sees more, and more people arriving to join in the fun. As midnight approaches all eyes turn to the magnificent sight of the castle, lit by flood-lights, and for the sounding of one of its cannons, high up on the castle ramparts. Usually a lone piper standing on the battlements plays a lament like 'My home' as the last few minutes tick by. Then as the New Year arrives the big castle gun fires which is the signal for a breath-taking firework display to begin, lighting up the midnight sky with one and a half tons of gunpowder. Shortly after, a pipe band strikes up some stirring tune like 'Scotland the

Brave' the crowds cheer before 'Auld Lang Syne' is sung and the celebrations continue on into the wee small hours.

Inverness

Although Edinburgh, being the capital city, draws a lot of the attention, other towns and cities across Scotland hold celebrations. Inverness, the capital of the Highlands, draws more than ten thousand revellers to its free Inverness Highland Hogmanay Street Party with the focus of much of its celebrations at Bught Park and Inverness's town centre. Referred to by some as 'Britain's biggest town' Inverness has a wonderfully relaxed and friendly feel. Built around the River Ness, with an eye-catching castle and ornate church, Inverness New Year's Eve celebrations sees the event bedecked with banners, bunting and tartan not to mention live music and festive lighting.

Aberdeen

The Granite City by the North Sea always gives the New Year a rousing welcome with many special events arranged in order to mark the occasion. In recent years the focus of the city's celebrations has been outside the Town House at the top of the city's principal thoroughfare - Union Street. As well as a firework display there is usually live music and other entertainment as midnight arrives in the city. Although it no longer has a castle on Castlehill complete with firing cannons, the city more than makes up for it in noise when the ships moored in its harbour all sound their horns and passing cars join in. There are of course lots of smaller celebrations too, going on across the city, in the many pubs and clubs where thousands of Hogmanay partygoers see in the New Year.

Stonehaven

At Stonehaven, just South of Aberdeen, there is the now famous Fireball Ceremony. Dating back many years the custom, at midnight, of around fifty fireball swingers celebrating the arrival of the New Year by whirling flaming balls of fire above their heads as they make their way through the old town continues to draw large crowds. This ceremony is repeated every year by locals to ward off evil spirits and to ensure good luck for the town.

Glasgow

As Scotland's largest city Glasgow is bustling with a wide variety of events and parties for Hogmanay. As well as its fantastic street party, centred around George Square, which annually attracts large crowds there are the numerous pubs, clubs, restaurants and hotels each with their own celebration. Although Glasgow's Hogmanay celebrations aren't, perhaps, quite as high profile as Edinburgh's they are nonetheless well worth the effort to visit and join in with.

Perthshire

Comrie in Perthshire has the ancient 'Flambeaux Procession' through the village to ward off evil spirits. These enormous torches, some ten feet high are prepared several weeks in advance and are brought out late on Hogmanay evening ready for midnight. Then, when the New Year arrives they are lit then raised aloft and carried shoulder high through the town, eventually being thrown into the River Earn to the cheers and laughter of the crowd and guisers

Moray Firth

At Burghead, on the Moray Firth, the locals celebrate the coming of the New Year by the 'Burning of the Clavie'. This ceremony takes place on January 1st of the old calendar or 'Auld Hogmanay', now the 11th and sees the 'clavie' – a barrel filled with tar, set alight and carried around the streets to purify the town and see off the old year. The custom ends with the clavie being taken to a hill where it burns on before members of the crowd pick pieces of the barrel as a symbol of good luck.

Lewis

On the Outer Hebridean Island of Lewis, Hogmanay is marked by a tradition that sees groups of boys carrying sticks and visiting each of the houses. They recite a rhyme in Gaelic before being invited in where one of the boys, who wears a sheep-skin walks clockwise around a chair in the house while members of the family hit the skin with sticks. On completing this good luck custom they are rewarded with some food, traditionally a bannock or oatcake.

These are, of course, just a few of the many events which occur each year all across the country and gives some idea of the fun and tradition associated with the celebration of Hogmanay and the arrival of the New Year in Scotland!

ESSENTIAL INGREDIENTS FOR A SCOTTISH HOGMANAY

Scotland's history, around 5000 years old, is a colourful and varied one. Hogmanay, along with Burns Night, is therefore seen by many Scots as a chance to celebrate their Scottishness, their history and their culture in a happy and passionate way. This means that, for many, the coming of Hogmanay is eagerly anticipated as a great night of fun, full of the traditional customs, food, music, drink and dress. To fully join in the Hogmanay experience means respecting the old ways for an evening, remembering why they were, and are, still important and discovering that we still have much in common with our ancestors.

Hogmanay Customs

Scotland like, any ancient nation, has it's superstitions and customs which shaped the way its country folk lived their lives. Being dependent on the land for their livelihood meant that good luck was seen to be a vitally important element to a family's continued success. This was especially true with the coming of New Year and its symbolic significance of renewal. Almost like planting a fresh year's crop Hogmanay, or New Year's Eve, was seen as sowing the seeds of your luck for the next twelve months, making it an important occasion if you wished to avoid a year of bad luck, ruined crops, sickly livestock and financial ruin. Therefore a series of customs, like 'first-footing' which we talk about later, became a vital safeguard to ensuring that evil spirits were kept away and another year's prosperity was ensured. Celebrating Hogmanay in true Scottish style means observing these customs and, as well as being good fun, who knows just how much good luck might come your way? We'll talk more about these important customs in later chapters.

Traditional Food

Scotland, due to its northern location had, traditionally, a very limited fare of foodstuffs for all but the very rich. Due to the many uprisings and battles both between clans and with the English much of the country's wealth diminished – times were hard for most folk and remained hard. This meant that much of the Scottish farmhouse food that we know so well today revolved around cheaper staples – such as oatmeal. Oatmeal was used to make lots of different foods including two of the best known, oatcakes and porridge. But with such a rich countryside with rivers full of salmon, glens with grouse and deer and seas brimming with haddock, mussels, prawns and even oysters – the opportunity to eat well was always there. True, this often meant that the poor were forced to poach in order to feed their families such food – running the risk of harsh treatment if caught. How Scotland prepares much of it's sea food can be attributed to the Viking raiders who introduced many of the techniques still in use today such as salting, curing and smoking of fish. The food detailed in later recipes is such traditional fare and can say more about old Scotland than a thousand words.

Whisky

What would Hogmanay be without a wee dram? An integral part of Hogmanay, whisky is also one of Scotland's best known exports. Essential for all Hogmanay parties a basic knowledge of this ancient drink becomes obligatory at this time of year – so what are the important things you should know? Firstly, the term 'whisky' is derived from the Gaelic phrase 'uisge beatha' or 'water of life'. Secondly, only whisky which is distilled and matured in Scotland for at least three years can carry the words 'Scotch Whisky' and unlike Ireland and the United States whisky is spelt without the 'e'. There are two main types of whisky namely 'malt' and 'grain'. 'Malt' whisky is made from malted barley and is widely regarded as the noblest of drinks. Of malt whisky there are two main types, a 'single malt' and a 'vatted malt'. A single malt is produced by only one distillery and means that whiskies of differing strengths and ages were mixed together - there is also the special 'single-cask malts' which are single malts but are bottled from only one cask making them rare and expensive. A vatted malt is where single malts of differing ages and from two or more distilleries are mixed together usually by blenders or large distillers with many different malts to their name. Grain whisky is used primarily in creating a blended whisky. Blended whisky, which is a mixture of malt and grain whiskies, is the most popular form of whisky with over a thousand varieties available. It is blended whisky that most people decide to buy due to its taste and affordability. When talking about whisky made in Scotland you should refer to it as either 'whisky' or 'Scotch whisky' and avoid referring to it as 'Scotch'.

Confused? If so don't worry, simply remembering the difference between a malt and a blend will help you avoid any obvious blunders when refilling a guest's glass.

Tartan

Tartan is one of the most well known patterns and fabrics in the world with a bewildering variety of colours and patterns. Wearing it at New Year and as part of a Hogmanay celebration always adds colour and charm to the occasion and with each Scottish clan having their own tartan which is used to make plaids, kilts and trousers (or 'trews' as they are known in Scotland) you're bound to find a tartan to suit you. Tartan also has an interesting history and was banned for thirty-five years by the Hanoverian Government after the 1745 Jacobite uprising of 'Bonnie Prince Charlie' or Charles Stewart was ended by the English victory at Culloden:

"That from and after the First Day of August, 1747, no Man or Boy, within that part of Britain called Scotland, other than such as shall be employed as Officers and Soldiers in His Majesty's Forces, shall, on any pretence whatsoever, wear or put on the Clothes commonly called Highland Clothes - that is to say - the Plaid, Philebeg, or Little Kilt, Trowse, Shoulder Belts, or any part whatsoever of what peculiarly belongs to the Highland Garb; and that no Tartan, or party-coloured Plaid or Stuff shall be used for Great Coats, or for Upper Coats..."

Although tartan can be worn in many forms it is most commonly associated with the wearing of the 'kilt'. The kilt or 'little kilt' as it was originally known, was a modification of the older 'belted plaid' a rectangular piece of cloth of 6 yards by 2 yards, splitting the lower half away from the top, flattening the front and stitching the pleats closed. For those wishing to wear tartan for the first time the important thing is to know which clan's tartan you should wear. This is decided by your surname e.g. a 'Stewart' will wear the 'Stewart' tartan. If your surname does not have a direct Scottish link you should look into your family background for other sur-

The knowledgeable might even don traditional garb...

names, most probably on your mother's side, which are no longer used. These names can then be checked against all the surnames that make up a clan and a suitable tartan found. Failing all that you can wear one of the most popular tartans 'Pride of Scotland' which was created for those without a family tartan.

The Clans

As mentioned, intrinsically linked with the wearing of tartan are the Scottish clans so a quick word on them is probably in order. The whole Highland way of life in Scotland was shaped by the clan system of living. The word 'clan' came from the Gaelic 'clann' meaning 'children' and this reflected the way the system worked. Each clan is descended from a single ancestor who gave the clan its name and so groups of people became linked together through marriage or ancestry. The clan chief was all-powerful and held his territory by the consent of the clan members who were his family, tenants and soldiers. Membership of a clan was essential and to be thrown out meant disgrace and dispossession. Each clan lived in a specific part of Scotland and there was bitter rivalry between differing clans resulting in many massacres. Clan members were summoned together by the 'Fiery Cross' which was carried through the clan's territory. The clan system is still respected in many parts of Scotland although it no longer carries the same vital importance it once did to one's survival.

Dancing

Scottish Highland dancing, one of the oldest forms of folk dancing, has been danced both by lords and the lower classes alike. With three distinct forms, solo, couple and set dances it continues to be danced at weddings and ceilidhs in Scotland and throughout the world. Of the solo dances the Highland Fling and Sword Dance are possibly the two most well known. With a fighting-related origin the Sword Dance or 'Gille Callum', for example, was a dance of victory, supposedly done at the end of a battle as the King danced in triumph over his blood soaked sword crossed with the captured sword of his dead opponent. Dances involving couples, such as the 'Gay Gordons' have been popular since the 1800's with set dances like the the Highland Reel still finding favour with modern Scots. We talk more about some of these dances later on and even show you how to dance them at your Hogmanay party.

Incorporating any or all of these essential ingredients will go a long way to giving your Hogmanay celebration that traditional feel. Spending a little time and effort preparing yourself for the coming of December the 31st need not become a major chore, many of the preparations are simple and straightforward, as the next chapter shows.

CHAPTER TWO

Getting Ready for Hogmanay

• •

Having a real Scottish Hogmanay celebration can be a great deal of fun. Firstly, you have all that wonderful, tried and tested tradition to add sparkle to the evening. Secondly, everyone wants to have a good time and are just looking for an opportunity to relax with other friends and enjoy themselves. To host any party, however, takes a little planning with any effort you can spend before Hogmanay being well worth it. After all you'll want to enjoy the party without running hither and thither due to lack of thought. Plan ahead and keep in mind that regardless of how many people you plan inviting numbers always tend to creep up above that level as friends bring guests who asked to come along. Once you've decided to hold a Hogmanay bash give yourself plenty of time to get organised so you can enjoy yourself too.

PLANNING YOUR HOGMANAY PARTY

How To Have A Great Party

Having a party and having a great party are two separate things altogether. There is a knack to throwing a good Hogmanay bash and much of it is

Stocking up with a few supplies...

common sense. So what can you do to help ensure yours falls into the latter category? Here are five useful hints.

- Firstly it is vital to have a 'host', a figure-head that sets the agenda for the evening, and moves events along if things look like they're slowing down a little. If you're not a natural raconteur then arrange for a friend or someone else to play the part of the M.C., to make announcements, to lead the first dance, show the steps, and generally to sparkle and shine. The host sets the tone for the Hogmanay party, if you're happy - then your party's likely to be a happy one too.

- Have an agenda. Sit down and make a list of events you plan to run during the evening, for example: food, dancing, party games, toasts, music requests, story telling, the arrival of the first foot etc. Plan to have plenty of things happening, even if you don't use them all, because you'll be hard pushed to try and think up things on the spot if there's a lull.

- Get guests to dress up. What better time to encourage men to don the kilt and for everyone to make the effort to dress in a traditional Highland manner? If, however, this isn't practical try and make it fancy dress. The very act of getting dressed up puts people in a party mood and makes breaking the ice so much easier as everyone starts talking by commenting on the costumes being worn.

✤   Make sure that all the adults get a drink when they arrive, if they want one that is, and, while no one wants a party full of mindless drunks, a few drinks will help most people feel less nervous and more like joining in the fun.

✤   Don't start the party too early. Remember your Hogmanay celebration will run, at least, an hour beyond midnight and probably well into the small hours so don't start too soon. If you're serving food give yourself a little longer, if you're just serving drinks make it later. It is far better to have a great party that finishes early than an average party that went on too long.

Sadly Dougie left his party preparations to chance.

Who should we invite?

Picking a balanced and compatible guest list is worth taking some time over. When considering an invitation to a party the first question most people will want to know is 'who else is going to be there?' With a whole host of social reasons behind whether or not people will want to turn up it is clearly sensible to pick your guests wisely. Try to go for a blend of people but err on the side of outgoing types who you know will want to participate in your Hogmanay party. Don't, however, make it too difficult for someone to refuse if they don't want to come - there's nothing worse than pushing a guest to come along only to find them sitting in a corner of the room with a glum face waiting to leave. Make up a provisional guest list and ask your friends what they think of your choice. They will no doubt suggest other names you may have forgotten or tell you if any of the guests you've picked won't get on. Avoid a 'boss' and 'employee' mix at all costs. Neither side will probably be able to really relax and enjoy themselves and if they do, usually via the assistance of drink, there is always the danger of people 'speaking their minds' – living to regret it and then blaming you for inviting the other person.

Where will you hold the Party?

Celebrating Hogmanay is inescapably linked with the home. All the 'good luck' customs and Hogmanay rituals are centred around the purification and preparation of the family home for the coming year. This means that holding your Hogmanay party at home is preferable to hiring a function room or some other venue for all but the largest of parties. When preparing your house remember the fewer guests you invite the more formal you can afford to make the party, i.e. sit-down dinner etc., if this is what you wish. The greater the number the more informal you are better making it with a buffet style set-up. As with any party you should clear away any furniture or ornaments that you are particularly fond of in order to avoid any accidental damage and make sure you have plenty of coasters, napkins and black bags handy which will help you keep any mess to a minimum.

Traditional Dress

Hogmanay's a great time to choose to wear Scotland's national costume and, surprisingly, there's actually very little etiquette surrounding the wearing of Highland dress. This means that it's a perfect choice for those wishing to add a touch of tradition and glamour to their Hogmanay party by making it a 'full Highland dress' affair. For those who don't own a kilt, and due to cost few do, dress hire shops commonly stock an impressive range of kilts and jackets or can usually arrange to get them for you through their trade contacts. It is wise, however, to give yourself and your guests as much advance warning as possible in order to allow them to get measured/fitted and to book their outfit well in advance of any last minute demand. So what's required to turn you into a highland lad or lassie?

For The Laddies

There are several parts to a standard outfit which are as follows: a short jacket, usually black; a black waistcoat (which, by the way, should never be removed); a white shirt and bow tie; a kilt in either of the two main kilt weights of 'regular' and 'heavyweight'; a sporran or pouch worn in front of kilt; a belt and buckle; white woollen socks with flashes; a Skean Dhu, or dagger tucked into sock and brogue 'Gillie' style shoes. Some people also like to wear the ancient 'fileadh-mor' with the tartan hung over the shoulder. Hats, although worn by some true enthusiasts, are not commonly worn by most men, primarily because they can give the outfit a somewhat military look and also because there is some important etiquette to remember before wearing one, especially surrounding the use of the cap badge.

For The Lassies

If there is relatively little etiquette with wearing the men's highland outfit then there is even less to worry about with the lady's attire. The key feature is the tartan sash, which is usually worn, in various arrangements with a long white evening dress - although it is often worn with any appropriate long evening dress. Another, some might say more eye-catching, alternative is to wear a long tartan kilt-skirt as shown in the illustration. The only area which gives rise to any argument relates to which shoulder the tartan sash should be worn over. Some say it has to be the left, others say the right depending on tradition and the status of the wearer. Clearly a decision has to be taken so it is probably best to wear it over the right shoulder unless told otherwise.

Your Quick Guide to Highland Dress

plaid brooch

'fileadh-mor'

short kilt jacket

black waist-coat beneath

sporran

kilt (worsted wool)

Long-laced brogue Gillie shoes

white woollen socks

sash brooch

white lace blouse with jabot

tartan sash

long, tartan kilt-skirt

Music

Choosing the right music can really ensure your Hogmanay celebration gets off to a good start. Have some soft music playing in the background before any of your guests arrive which will help set the mood and, as the evening progresses, you can start playing more traditional Scottish music turning the volume up as the party begins to take off.

Scottish music is perfect for any party but is essential for Hogmanay parties, especially where dancing is involved. The tunes are short, easy to listen to and very catchy. There is usually a good, strong beat which makes dancing in time to the music, especially if you're learning a new step, much easier and enjoyable. Visit your local music store if you don't have any Scottish country music records, or ask your friends if they or their relatives have any suitable records.

You may, however, be lucky enough to have someone to play the piano for you or you may even plan to hire a band. If so you can give them the sheet music for the two dances featured in this book, although they'll probably have them already, and nothing beats good live music. Whatever you do make sure you have the music for the two dances featured as these songs fit the steps better than any other.

Try out the music before the party, play it at party level (neighbours permitting) and decide what tunes work the best. You may also find you need to borrow extra speakers depending on how big the party is going to be. When you've decided, arrange the records, discs or tapes in the order you're going to play them and have them at the side of the hi-fi. You'll want to keep the party atmosphere going and that means keeping the music going, so make sure you have enough songs to last, without having to repeat them again. If you can, try putting someone in charge of the music so that you can keep an eye on other things.

Piping In The New Year

If you'd like to give your Hogmanay bash a real touch of class why not arrange for a piper to arrive just before midnight to make a big entrance and to 'skirl' the old year out and the new one in. Perhaps you know a bagpipe playing friend who can do this for you or you may have to hire a professional to turn up and do the honours. If your party's big (and important) enough, you could try making contact with a Scots regiment, perhaps based locally or on a tour of duty, and be fortunate enough to have the presence of an army piper resplendent in full military attire. More than likely you'd want to invite the piper and his friends and family along with the promise of some money, free food, drink and a lot of good fun. At any rate be sure to keep their arrival a secret and watch the faces of your guests light up when the music begins! You'll need time to arrange this so book someone well in advance.

Sending Out Your Invitations

Finally when sending out invitations or calling by telephone to invite someone remember they've probably got, or soon will have, a choice of other New Year's Eve parties to attend. Why should they come along to yours? This is where your planning and effort will make all the difference in the sort of people you can attract along and how long they will want to stay. Unlike most other parties which rely on an ad-hoc, or what'll we do?, approach yours will be truly themed and well planned. You will be able to tempt guests with something traditional and a little special. Not to mention some fine food, it's worth mentioning a few of the courses that'll be on offer, as well as some unusual drinks and a whole evening's worth of Scottish good-will party culture!

PREPARING SOME TRADITIONAL FOOD FOR HOGMANAY

What's On The Menu?

With so many traditional Scottish dishes to choose from you are never really stuck for choice. Produce from Scotland, due to it's largely unspoilt and beautiful countryside, is nearly always of the highest possible standard. Our menu has many of the traditional dishes which are suitable for either a buffet or 'sit-down' dinner party. Some of these dishes, especially the puddings, as well as a few of the drinks are best prepared well in advance of Hogmanay. This means that much of the work can be completed before the big day arrives, thereby cutting down on much of the grind involved with setting up the party.

Soups
Scotch Broth
Lentil Soup

Cold Foods for the Sideboard
Haunch of Venison
Scotch Eggs
Salmon Sandwiches
Various cold cooked meats
Meat Roll
Cheeses

Main Courses
Haggis, served with turnips & mashed potatoes
Stovies & Oatcakes

Pudding
Cranachan
Black Bun

Biscuits & Cakes
Shortbread
Dundee Cake

The Drinks Menu
Cherry Brandy
Het Pint
Ginger Wine
Whisky
Highland Mead
Atholl Brose
Winter Brew

Ten minutes before the guests arrive...

...and another triumph in the kitchen

Lentil Soup

Ingredients
½ lb lentils
1 Onion
Chopped pieces of carrot and turnip
2-3 sticks of celery
1 oz of dripping
2 quarts of water or stock
Salt, pepper, baking soda

Preparing
Wash lentils
Boil some water add a good pinch of baking soda and leave lentils overnight.
Rinse and drain the lentils from water.
Cut vegetables into small cubes or thin slices.
Melt the dripping in pan, add lentils and vegetables, and sweat until the fat is absorbed.
Add water and salt.
Bring slowly to the boil.
Simmer for up to 2½ hours until vegetables are cooked.
Season to taste and serve.

Scotch Broth

Ingredients
2 lb shin of beef
2 quarts of cold water
1 teacupful of diced carrot
1 teacupful of diced turnip
3 leeks sliced
2 ozs of barley

2 ozs of green peas
1/4 of cabbage (shredded)
1 grated carrot
1 tablespoon of chopped parsley
Salt and pepper.

Preparing
Wash and soak peas overnight.
Clean and trim meat before placing it in a pan with cold water.
Add the peas.
Add the barley, well washed.
Add the salt and bring quickly to boiling point, skimming throughout.
Add well-washed and prepared vegetables (except the grated carrot and chopped parsley) to the meat and simmer slowly for 3 to 4 hours.
About 20 minutes before serving, add the grated carrot, and allow to cook.
Five minutes before serving add chopped parsley, season well and serve piping hot.

Meat Roll
Ingredients
½ lb stewing steak
¼ lb fat bacon
3 ozs bread-crumbs
1 egg
¼ of a pint of stock or water
Pinch of allspice
Salt & pepper
Browned bread crumbs

Preparing

Heat a pan of boiling water with a few vegetables in it for flavour.

Clean meat and bacon and pass it through mincer twice.

Add breadcrumbs, seasonings and beaten egg, and mix well.

Form into a roll, place in a cloth and tie ends of cloth securely.

Place in the boiling water and boil steadily for 3 hours.

When ready, re-wrap in a clean cloth before cooling between two plates, with a good weight on top to press into shape.

Remove cloth and toss in browned crumbs before serving with salad.

Haggis

Scotland's most famous dish. Associated primarily with Burn's Night (25th January, his birthday) but great for any time of the year especially New Year! Although true devotees usually make their own haggis there are many fine pre-prepared ones available these days. To cook place into a pot and cover with water. Bring to the boil then reduce the heat and allow to simmer with the lid on for three hours. Make sure not to overboil the haggis as this may cause it to burst. Serve hot with turnips and mashed potatoes.

Stovies

Ingredients

2 ozs butter
3 medium onions, roughly chopped
2 lbs of thickly sliced potatoes
1 teaspoon of salt
¼ teaspoon of black pepper, ground
1 handful of any leftover chopped meat
1 tablespoon of chives
1 cup of stock

Preparing
Melt butter in a heavy-based pan.
When hot add sliced onions.
Reduce heat and cook gently until golden brown.
Add potatoes making sure they are well coated.
Add salt and pepper.
Add stock and cook for about half an hour.
Add meat and chives.
Simmer for another quarter of an hour.
Serve with oatcakes.

Oatcakes
Ingredients
8 oz medium oatmeal
8 oz fine oatmeal
1 teaspoon caster sugar
½ teaspoon baking powder
½ teaspoon salt
2 ozs melted butter
½ cup hot water

Preparing
Preheat your oven to 180C

Prepare a couple of oven trays with baking paper.
Mix oatmeals and add baking powder, sugar and salt
together in a fairly large bowl.
Add melted butter and hot water.
Work into a firm dough.
Place dough on a flat surface dusted with oatmeal.
Roll out into a square about ¼" thick adding extra
oatmeal if necessary to prevent sticking.
Cut into squares.
Place squares onto trays allowing ½" all around for
expansion and bake for 25 minutes.
Remove from oven and allow to cool before moving
from cooking trays.

Cranachan

Ingredients
2 large tablespoons oatmeal
1 cup of double cream
whisky, rum or vanilla
Raspberries, strawberries or other soft fruit
sugar

Preparing
Toast the oatmeal in a pan on a low heat for 5 min-
utes.
Whisk the cream until stiff then add the sugar.
Add the oatmeal to the cream but avoid making mix-
ture too thick.
Layer into a tall dessert glass, raspberries and
cream.
Add whisky or rum etc., and flavour to taste.
Chill for half and hour before serving.

Black Bun

Ingredients

12½ ozs raisins
10 ozs currants
2½ cups of plain flour
6 ozs butter
1 tablespoon of caster sugar
1 teaspoon of crystal sugar
2 tablespoons of water
2 egg yolks
3½ ozs of mixed peel, dried
3½ ozs of flaked almonds
½ cup of buttermilk
¾ cup of plain flour
1 egg and yolk whisked lightly
1 egg white whisked lightly
1 teaspoon of ground ginger
1 teaspoon of cinnamon
1 teaspoon of allspice
1 small dash of whisky
¼ teaspoon of cream of tartar
½ cup of buttermilk
¼ teaspoon of bicarbonate of soda
¾ cup of castor sugar

Preparing

Prepare a loaf tin with some oil.
Take flour, butter and sugar and mix in a food processor until fine.
Add water and egg yolks and mix until dough is soft.
Cover bowl with food wrap and place in fridge for 20 minutes.

Take a mixing bowl and add fruit, peel, almonds, sugar spices and whisky.

Mix.

Take a sieve and add flour, bicarbonate of soda and cream of tartar onto fruit.

Add milk.

Add egg.

Add egg yolk.

Mix well until bound together.

Take two thirds of the pastry from fridge and roll out until large enough to cover base and sides of loaf tin. Leave ¾" of pastry for a seal.

Tip fruit mix into tin and press out to fill.

Take left over pastry from fridge and roll out until big enough to cover top of bun.

Take egg white and brush onto top of fruit and edges of pastry in tin.

Cover tin with rolled out pastry and firmly press the edges together to seal.

Trim surplus pastry around side of tin.

Use egg white to coat top of bun then dust with a coating of sugar.

Place in a preheated oven 180C for an hour.

Now reduce heat to 160C for another hour and a half.

Bun should be nicely brown when finished.

Allow to cool before removing from tin.

Shortbread

Ingredients
6 ozs flour
2 ozs rice flour

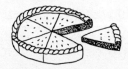

Pinch of salt
4 ozs butter
2 ozs castor sugar

Preparing
Grease a tin and paper it.
Mix the dry ingredients and add all the butter.
Blend the flour and sugar with the butter until a consistency of short crust is attained.
Turn out onto a board and shape into a round cake about ¾ inch thick.
Use fork to score the edges all round and prick the top well.
Place on baking tray put in moderate oven for around an hour.

Dundee Cake
Ingredients
4 eggs
2 ozs plain flour
6 ozs butter
6 ozs caster sugar
6 ozs self-raising flour
pinch of salt
12 ozs of sultanas & currants
3 ozs of halved, blanched almonds
1 tablespoon of grated orange peel

Preparing
Wash and prepare fruit
Blend the butter and sugar until light and fluffy.
Adding eggs one at a time along with a little flour to

stop curdling.
Mix in half the flour and add the salt.
Mix in orange peel, sultanas and currants along with
rest of the flour.
Gently mix until bound together.
Empty into lined and greased baking tin and deco-
rate with almonds on top.
Bake for an hour at 180C before reducing tempera-
ture to 150C for up to another hour and a half.

HOGMANAY DRINKS

Having a good and varied supply of soft and alco-
holic drink is vital. Clearly if you're planning on
inviting a large number of guests the cost can quickly mount up, if this is a problem simply ask your
guests to follow the common practice of 'bringing a
bottle' with them. This can be mentioned if you're
inviting your guests by telephone or included on
their invitation card – if possible, specify what you'd
like them to bring which will avoid everyone turning
up with the same thing. Should you feel uncomfort-
able about asking your guests you can fall back on
the tried and tested 'Winter Brew' mentioned later
on. This delicious drink is perfect for most guests'
tastes and a plentiful supply can be prepared cheap-
ly and will ensure much 'good cheer' throughout the
evening. Supplement this with a supply of beer and
a few popular spirits and your drinks bill shouldn't
be too excessive.
    Many guests will, no doubt, be quite content to

sip away at their favourite tipple throughout the evening, but, as it is a special occasion, why not encourage the willing to try something just a little bit unusual by preparing some or all of the following. These drinks are quick and easy to make, taste great and will add a little je ne sais quoi to your drinks list.

Cherry Brandy

This is a marvellous drink, sweet and very drinkable. In many ways this is it's biggest drawback so make sure your guests are aware of this and ration themselves accordingly - if they want to be fairly sober when midnight strikes that is! Prepare well in advance and allow to mature - the longer the better.

Ingredients
1/2 lb of castor sugar
1 large bottle of cherry syrup
1 ltr of Bulmer's cider
1 gill of brandy

Preparing
Add ingredients to a container and stir until sugar is melted in the bottle. The longer you can leave the mixture to mature the better.

Het Pint

The Het or 'hot' pint has particular Hogmanay significance being a form of traditional punch much favoured at New Year and especially suitable with traditional Hogmanay fare. Make sure not to boil the mixture as this will evaporate the alcohol.

Ingredients
1 pint of whisky
8 pints of mild ale
6 eggs, well beaten
2 tablespoons of nutmeg
8 ozs of sugar

Preparing
Empty ale into a deep cooking pot.
Mix in nutmeg and heat until it's nearly at the boil
Stir in sugar until dissolved.
Slowly add eggs taking care not to curdle.
Add the whisky and again bring nearly to the boil.
Pour from one heated pot to another till liquid becomes clear and bright.

Ginger Wine

A tasty, non-alcoholic drink quick to prepare and suitable for those who don't want anything stronger.
Ingredients
1 orange
1 lemon
1 oz of root ginger
½ gl of water
1 ½ lb of sugar
1 pinch of pepper

Preparing
Slice up orange and lemon.

Add water to a cooking pot.
Add ingredients.
Boil mixture, strain and bottle.

Whisky

Whisky is an essential for any Hogmanay party and many prefer to drink it like it is so ensure you have both a good malt and good blend available for the true connoisseurs. For those who don't like it straight why not try this whisky cocktail but make sure you use a blend not a malt or no Scot will ever be able to forgive you.

An 'Old Fashioned'

Ingredients
90ml of whisky (blended)
Bitters
1 teaspoon of castor sugar
3-4 ice cubes

Preparing
Put sugar into glass and add two dashes of bitters before mixing with the spoon. Add ice cubes and whisky.

Highland Mead

This very strong drink, made from honey and water which has been fermented with yeast, has been known since ancient times and is believed to have been introduced to Scotland by the Norse raiders the Vikings. This drink is best prepared some months in advance and left to mature. Be careful not to drink too much, it's very potent!

Ingredients
1 pint of honey to every 3 pints of water
1 sachet of yeast, as found in any home-brew beer making kit

Preparing
Using a large pot heat the water while adding the honey
Bring to boil for five minutes
Switch off heat and allow to cool to 37 C
Sprinkle in yeast and stir
Carefully transfer to a fairly large container (one that will fit into your fridge later on)
Seal with lid, allowing room for expansion through fermentation
Store in the dark place (e.g. a cupboard) for about a week
Now put container into your refrigerator and allow to cool for about three days
When mixture settles remove from fridge, strain to remove sediment, bottle
Place bottles into a cool, dark place and allow to mature.

Atholl Brose

An old Scots drink with several colourful tales about its origins but all tales reflect its intoxicating nature. The only thing you need remember is always to shake bottle well before pouring.

Ingredients
2 pints of Scotch Whisky
2 cups of water
3 heaped tablespoons of oatmeal
2 tablespoons of runny honey

Preparing
Take a bowl empty oatmeal into it and add water.
Mix well then leave for twenty minutes to half an hour.
Strain mixture through a sieve into a bowl.
This will leave you with just the oatmeal-water.
Add honey to oatmeal-water and mix in well.
Funnel into a quart bottle.
Fill the rest of the bottle with whisky and seal.

'Winter Brew'

If you're serving a buffet then what better way to have drink available, without personally having to pour every glass, than by providing a punch bowl. This delicious winter brew will warm the coldest of arriving guests - perfect for those chilly Scottish nights and is very cheap and easy to prepare. Just make sure you don't boil the mixture when preparing and it'll taste great.

Ingredients
5 fl ozs ruby port
3 fl ozs of brandy
Bottle of Red Wine
3 fl ozs Triple Sec
3 cinnamon sticks

3 sliced Lemons
3 sliced Oranges
3 sliced Limes

Preparing
Mix ingredients in a pot and slowly heat only until simmering, not boiling. Switch off heat and allow to cool for about quarter of an hour before serving in a punch bowl.

AVOIDING THE HOGMANAY HANGOVER

While we're on the subject of alcohol it is perhaps prudent to mention this subject before the actual day arrives. For although Hogmanay can be a wonderful celebration and the parties surrounding it a highlight to the end of any year – for most of us there is the inevitable risk of suffering the Hogmanay Hangover. Generally, with no work to go to the next day along with the fun-filled, party atmosphere there is always the temptation to push the boat out a little too far and have a few drinks too many. It's not really such an auspicious start to any year to awaken, sometime in the late morning, feeling rather the worse for wear and praying for someone to stop ringing the bells in your head. Firstly, there is no quick-fix cure to a hangover once you have one but you can do much to minimise the likelihood and severity of any ill effects by following some simple advice before, and during, an evening's festivities.

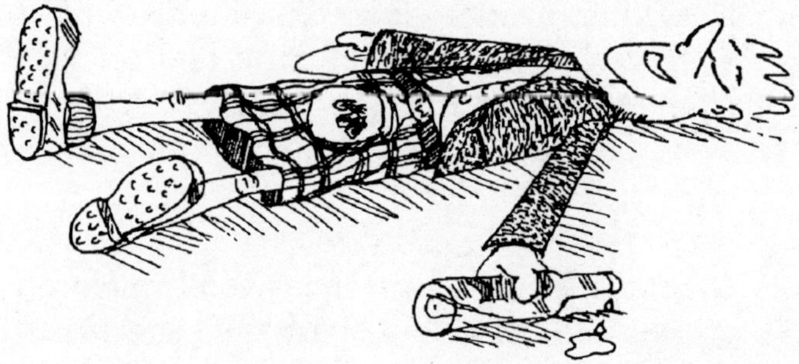

At parties, Hamish takes his drink-serving role very seriously and selflessly insists on sampling each bottle for quality...

- Eating before you start to party is essential. Food slows down the body's absorption of alcohol and helps protect the lining of the stomach.

- Smoking makes you want to drink more so, if possible, cut down during the evening - this is because alcohol makes veins and arteries expand while nicotine makes them contract - which is why the two seem to go together so well, until the next morning that is!

- Follow the old saying "don't mix the grape and the grain". If you're 'drinking the grape' i.e. wine, cognac etc., try to stick to those drinks and similarly if 'favouring the grain' i.e. beer and whisky keep to those. Keep in mind the darker and sweeter the drink the more likely it will be to induce a hangover.

- Drinking orange juice, and other freshly squeezed citrus fruits during and after your Hogmanay party will provide you with valuable Vitamin C which helps to neutralise the effects of alcohol.

- Drinking plenty of water, especially before you go to sleep, will help the body cope with the dehydrating effects of the alcohol and reduce stomach acid.

- Remember, unthinkable though it may seem to some you are allowed to say 'no thanks' when being plyed with yet another refill.

- Finally, if you can manage it, eating a good New Year's Day breakfast the will help restore the body's blood sugar levels and reduce any drowsiness, faintness and trembling you're feeling.

CHAPTER THREE

Hogmanay's Here

• •

Some Hogmanay & New Year's Day parties begin early and last for three to four days, or sometimes longer depending on how eager the guests are to celebrate. For most people though, the two day's of Hogmanay and New Year's day are more than enough to have all the fun and excitement you can handle.

HOGMANAY CUSTOMS

Purifying the House

Cleanliness and untidiness at New Year are two things certain to bring bad luck on a household. To counter this, in olden days, women spent many, many days cleaning the house to make it ready for the coming year. Pots would be scrubbed, rooms dusted, tables washed until the whole home was as clean as a new pin. The men too would be kept busy hurrying around fin-  ishing chores about the house or farm so that by midnight on Hogmanay their dwelling was ready for the New Year and could not be found wanting.

A few of the lads 'pop round' for a quiet drink...

Settling Debts

Beginning a New Year encumbered by debts from a previous year was, and still is by custom, something to be avoided. Whether purely financial or a debt 'in kind', in days gone by the debtor would make strenuous efforts to pay off their dues in whole, or as fully as they could, so that they could begin the following year with a clean slate. While being a good principal for those who could avoid to settle it would often see those who couldn't, scraping together all they could to repay their loan only to borrow the money again as soon as the New Year arrived. Still, this satisfied the ritual and avoided any bad luck. These days there would be financial chaos across the world if banks and investment houses followed this custom, but on a personal level it would go some way to stopping increasing debts if more of us did clear our feet of such monetary worries each year.

Putting Aside Old Scores

Following the superstitious belief in the renewal of all things, including the soul, during the Hogmanay and New Year period there is also the custom of forgiving and forgetting old enmities. Most probably Christian in origin the arrival of the New Year was supposed to be an opportunity for local people to end their differences and begin afresh as good neighbours. While highly unlikely in the modern cities of today in the older rural communities of the past this is, perhaps, not as far-fetched as it sounds. With the first-footing custom being closely observed, not to mention a strong melancholy brought on by drink, it is more than likely that warring parties would be brought together by other locals so they could settle their differences and, thus, restore good order to the community – until the next 'falling out' that is!

Chasing Away the Evil Spirits

The last thing you want is to begin a New Year with all the old and evil spirits still with you. These malevolent entities accumulate during the year and can ruin your future prosperity if not chased away before, and during, the New Year's arrival. Luckily there are two main weapons to use against these, somewhat cowardly, evil sprites. Light and noise are sure fire ways of sending them packing and are best used in combination with each other to ensure that come midnight your home is free from any unwelcome phantoms. Therefore, come midnight put all the house lights on, open the windows and doors and make plenty of noise with which to chase away such spirits.

IT'S PARTY TIME!

The party spirit can start early in Scotland but it's best if it doesn't start too early. Nine o'clock on Hogmanay evening is probably as early as you'd want to kick things off, so don't be persuaded otherwise by over eager guests. When guests arrive offer them a dram and you can begin by explaining some of the things that will be happening during the course of the evening so that as midnight draws nearer they can be ready for them. It's also a good time to talk about the menu of traditional food you'll be serving and to start some of the guests off on two of the most popular Scottish dances.

Highland Dancing

One of the oldest forms of folk dance, Highland Dancing is great for really getting a party going. With its military origins reflected in such dances as the Highland Fling and The Sword Dance the all-male, fighting- related nature of Highland Dancing has given way to the more peaceful, but nonetheless enjoyable steps we know today. There are, of course, many wonderful dances but the two we are going to look at are simple to do and even if no one's tried them before you can all have a lot of fun by quickly learning the steps. At the end of the night though, you'll probably know them off by heart and can learn a few more if you so wish. The dances we'll look at are called 'The Gay Gordons' and 'The St Bernard's Waltz'. Both dances need partners, the first dance is faster, the second a slower more restful one.

The Dance of the Gay Gordons

A very simple and popular dance attributed to the proud and courageous northeast Scotland regiment, the Gordon Highlanders. The word 'gay' in this instance was used in the old sense meaning 'happy'

Forming up

In pairs begin by forming a big circle around the room, with the men standing to the left side of their

Dancing the 'Gay Gordons'

partners, holding 'hand over shoulder' man's left hand crossing his chest to hold his partner's left hand, his right hand crossing over her shoulder to hold her raised right hand.

Beginning the dance
To begin walk four steps forward, half turn and walk three steps backwards. You are now facing the place where you began.

Repeat this again by walking four steps forward, half turn and three steps backwards. You should now be back in the same place you started.

The Gay Gordons

Walking forward with partners holding right hands, she 'birls' or twirls four times under the man's arm. At the end of the fourth birl take up a waltz position and do three full turns.

Repeat. Four steps forward, half turn...

St Bernard's Waltz
Our second dance is somewhat slower than the first but is still very popular nevertheless.

Forming up
Begin by adopting the standard waltz hold men facing the wall, women the centre of the room.

Beginning the dance
Couples start by gliding three steps to the gentleman's left (his partner's right) and stepping twice on the spot for the fourth beat.

Now glide two steps to the gentleman's right before gliding two steps backwards towards the centre of the room. Man then glides two steps forward while his partner glides two steps back.

Man places left foot to side and crosses his right foot

The St Bernard's
Waltz

over left while his partner turns below his right arm.

Now waltz three full turns before repeating all the steps again remembering to keep in time with the music.

Serving The Food

Whilst you may have provided some light snacks, with a 9 p.m. start to a Hogmanay party you'll probably want to start serving the hot food around 10:30pm. This can be done either to a set, sit down dinner or to a more relaxed buffet style, depending on how formal or informal you wish the event to be. Buffet style is probably easiest as Hogmanay is not traditionally an occasion for a great deal of dining etiquette by the majority of Scots but the choice is yours. It's good, hearty, traditional fare and very tasty too so be prepared for requests for second helpings by some of your guests.

PARTY GAMES

Between spells of dancing, or, indeed, for those who don't care to dance but wish to join in some of the fun, party games are always sure to brighten up the atmosphere. These three games are easy to play, don't require elaborate props so can be played straight away.

The Two Minute Speech

Prepare a series of funny or fairly obscure speech

titles on different pieces of paper. Now a volunteer chooses one of them and gets twenty seconds to think a little about the title they've picked. Then the title is announced by the organiser to the other guests before the volunteer stands up and, facing the group, tries to give a fluent two-minute talk about the topic they have chosen. Laughing or long pauses are not allowed and everyone must be able to hear them. At the end of two minutes there can be thirty seconds of questions.

Once everyone playing has given a speech there should be a vote for the best speaker who then wins a prize.

Playing Hints
Don't pick anything too obscure or difficult as players will lose interest, for example 'The Inside of a Light Bulb' is not an easy subject for most people. Instead try some of the following favourites "If I Were In Charge I'd...", "The Problem With Society Is..." etc.

Spin The Bottle
Our next game requires everyone to form a circle of chairs around an empty bottle. Players take their seats while the organiser, or "Bottle Spinner", stands in the centre and explains the rules.

Everyone has to think up an exciting opening sentence to a story, for example it might be "The mad scientist realised only too late that his experiment was going seriously wrong..."

Now the Bottle Spinner spins the bottle and whoever it points to begins with their opening sentence, while they are speaking the bottle is spun again and the next speaker has to continue the story from where the last person left it.

Anyone taking too long to continue the story is out and everyone must be ready to stop mid-sentence to let the next person take over.

Spot The Difference

With a fairly large group of people someone is chosen to be the 'spotter'. Everyone else lines up whereupon the spotter is given thirty seconds to memorise the appearance of the other players.

The spotter then leaves the room for another thirty seconds to allow the others to change some things about their appearance. For example they may swap jumpers, turn-up the bottoms of their trousers, undo a button etc., before the spotter is called back in to then try and name as many changes as they can within one minute. Another spotter can then be chosen.

MINUTES TO MIDNIGHT

Final Toasts for the Old Year and For The New Year to Come!

It's been great fun but look, the clock draws near the hour and midnight is nearly upon us. It's important to make sure everyone is ready and that their glasses are all full so they can toast the New Year when it arrives. Now you have a few moments to bid farewell to the old year and to prepare for the new. This would be a good time to take out your big sheet of card with the words to Auld Lang Syne written on it and place or pin it somewhere in clear view. Next you should offer toasts to the old year, a very old traditional toast is:

"Rise up, guid wife, and shak yir feathers:
Dinna think that we are beggars:
We're only guid folks come to play:
Rise up and gie's oor Hogmanay!"

or

"Rise up, goodwife, and shake your feathers:
Do not think that we are beggars:
We're only good folks come to play
Rise up and give us our Hogmanay!"

Here's another fine toast that wishes you always to be as happy as possible:

"May the best you've ever seen
Be the worst you'll ever see;
May the mouse ne'er leave your girnal
Wi' a tear drap in its e'e;
May your lum keep blithely reekin'
Till your auld enough to dee;
May you aye be just as happy
As I wish you now to be!"

And finally here's a toast for everyone with links to

Scotland who can't be there for Hogmanay but miss it still:

My heart's in the Highlands, my heart is not here;
My heart's in the Highlands a-chasing the deer;
Chasing the wild deer, and following the roe,
My heart's in the Highlands, wherever I go.

Robert Burns.

The Last Minutes...

Now with the clock sweeping round everyone should start to make as much noise as they can, this is to scare away any evil spirits that might be lingering to mar the coming year. Then, with ten seconds to go everyone should count the seconds away. Ten, nine, eight, seven, six, five, four, three, two, one...

CHAPTER FOUR

Happy New Year To One An A'!

●●●●●●●●●●●●●●●●●●●●●●●●●●●●●●●●●●

Feliz año nevo!

Ein gluckliches neues jahr!

Gelukkig niewjaar!

Gott nyatt år!

FELIZ ANO NOVO!

Bonne année!

Felice anno nuovo!

Bliadhna Mhath ur!

Yes, the old year's been rung out and the New Year lies before us. As we've said this is an important moment according to tradition for your year's luck hangs in the balance at this time. Therefore you will be eagerly awaiting a knock on your door from your 'first foot'. This man, for it has to be a man, brings with him your luck for the year so you'll have to keep an open ear to hear him or, more conveniently, you could always arrange a set time for him to arrive. More about first-footing in a moment though. In the meantime it has become the custom, in many parts of the world, to sing 'Auld Lang Syne' just after midnight. This old Scottish tune, known as 'The Miller's Wedding' and 'The Miller's Daughter' was in print since 1700 but the poet Robert Burns wrote down, what he termed the 'old song of the olden times' from an old man's

singing about 1789. 'Auld Lang Syne' means 'old long ago' and is a song of friendship and remembrance.

Auld Lang Syne

Should auld acquaintance be forgot,
And never brought to mind?
Should auld acquaintance be forgot,
And auld lang syne?

Chorus
For auld lang syne, my dear
For auld lang syne
We'll tak a cup o kindness yet,
For auld lang syne!

(Cross hands)
And surely ye'll be your pint-stowp,
And surely I'll be mine,
And we'll take a cup o kindness yet,
For auld lang syne!

Repeat Chorus

We twa hae run about the braes,
And pou'd the gowans fine,
But we've wander'd monie a weary fit,
Sin auld lang syne

Repeat Chorus

We twa hae paidl'd in the burn
Frae morning sun till dine,
But seas between us braid hae roar'd

Sin auld lang syne

Repeat Chorus

And there's a hand my trusty fiere,
And gie's a hand o thine
And we'll tak a right guid-willie waught,
For auld lang syne

Repeat Chorus

Those singing 'Auld Lang Syne' should form a circle and hold hands while they sing the first verse and chorus. At the beginning of verse two they should cross arms in the traditional manner to symbolically 'shake' hands with the person on their left while they are singing.

Some say that the 'crossing' of hands should be left to the final verse to co-incide with that verse's words but for many people, who don't know all about the song, the impulse to cross hands as soon as possible is very strong. Rather than spoil the mood of the party by being too pedantic suggest verse two - for well-trained party members cross arms for verse five.

FOLLOWING SCOTLAND'S NEW YEAR'S DAY CUSTOMS

Until the 18th Century the first of January was the day of the year to give gifts, even more so than

Christmas Day. Although this practice is no longer widely observed it does continue on through the custom of 'first footing', but more of this in a moment -but first we have to ensure the house is free from unwanted spirits.

Chasing Away the Evil Spirits – Part II
Just in case there are any particularly stubborn spirits still lingering it is wise, once midnight has arrived to throw open the windows of the house and to, again, make as much noise as you can to convince any remaining evil demons to be on their way. It is worth pointing out that in this modern day of noise pollution laws and bureaucrats you may be forced, according to where you live, to watch the level and duration of any 'din' you can make. Certainly a few moments at midnight when most people are cheering will be more than ample time to complete the custom and should avoid you falling foul of any unwanted complaints.

Nothing Must Leave
Once midnight has been struck nothing must leave the house until the first foot arrives bringing with him his good luck and gifts. To break this rules will mean a year of lost possessions, poor fortunes and much bad luck. In many places in Scotland this custom extended to the whole of New Year's day just to be on the safe side, so be warned.

First Footing
Of all the traditions first footing is the single most

important custom during the Hogmanay and New Year period. With the 'first foot' (meaning the 'first foot to cross the threshold of the house') comes all the family's good luck or bad luck for that year. This is why, in many parts of Scotland prior arrangements are made for a suitable 'first foot' to call on the house at a pre-arranged time. To ensure good luck the first footer should be a tall, healthy, handsome, dark-haired man with an honest, good nature and generous personality. He must NOT arrive empty handed but should bring with him four things. A lump of coal or peat to symbolise the continued supply of fuel for the family's needs; some silver, this is usually some coins which helps bring prosperity and wealth; a Black Bun ensuring the family will always have food to eat and finally he should also bring with him a bottle of whisky with which to toast the household. It is thought that the origins of first-footing comes from Norse folklore and this Scandinavian connection may also explain why the custom dictates that the man should not be blond but 'dark' – possibly reflecting the fear the ancient Scots had of the blond warrior Vikings who once raided their coast. Other 'unlucky' first footers are said to be people with flatfeet, cross-eyes, eyebrows that join in the middle and even women with red hair!

Anytime after midnight has been struck by the clock the first foot can arrive. He should knock on the door which should be opened by the head of the household. Nothing should be said until the first foot has entered the house and placed the peat or coal in the fireplace. He should then pour a dram (drink) for the head of the house and while he drinks it down should then toast the house with a suitable phrase such as:

"God bless this house!"

or

"Bi suthainn!" (pronounced be-soothan, meaning 'Be prosperous')

The head of the house should then return the gesture by pouring a drink for the first foot. After this a glass of whisky should be offered, again by the head of the house, to his wife then to all the women. The husband then tops it up for every sip drunk then passes it to the men.

With the good luck for the coming year assured the first foot can then claim a kiss from every woman in the house as his reward.

Turn No One Away

Highland hospitality is now something of a legend. Many are the old stories of unfortunate travellers who arrived at a Highland croft in desperate need of help and were welcomed in, given warmth, food, drink and a bed for the night even though the people were often very poor and could ill afford to be so generous. For Hogmanay there is also the added significance of renewing friendships and forgetting old scores. This 'amnesty' period is therefore sacrosanct and those closing the door on a guest, whether sought or not, bring on themselves much bad luck.

"Taking the Cream Off the Water"

Next we have a tradition, especially favoured in Galloway on the West coast of Scotland, 'taking the cream off the water' or 'creaming of the well' is a practice said to bestow wonderfully good luck on those fortunate enough to taste the first water drawn from a well on New Year's Day. Although a practice not widely followed throughout the rest of Scotland these days it is said to ensure marriage between an unwed couple if both sip from the water before midnight making it especially suitable for courting couples.

Resolutions

Another important custom is the making of your New Year's resolution. It is wise to give this some careful thought and when you're ready it should be announced to others in order to commit yourself to it. Ideally you should make your resolution within the first day of the New Year, for obvious reasons, as this symbolises a new beginning and is said to hold more good luck.

The making of resolutions, like celebrating New Year, also dates back to the early Babylonians, but unlike our modern resolutions, like dieting or stopping smoking, the Babylonian's most popular pledge was the very mundane one of *returning borrowed farming equipment!* For most people these days their resolutions revolve around giving up bad habits

Father makes his annual resolutions...

or promising to do good things in the coming year. However, in recent years, only about fifty percent of people have bothered to make a New Year's resolution and only about half actually succeed in sticking to their pledge. This lack of commitment , it seems, is greatest amongst the older population who perhaps feel disheartened by previous year's failures, but the young seem keener to make the effort and as a result have greater success sticking with their resolutions.

Popular Resolutions to Make (or break)

Lose weight
Stop smoking
Improve my diet
Drink less
Try to be happier
Exercise more
Stay out of debt
Get a better job
Learn to drive
Stop swearing
Save up more money
Socialise more
Take up a hobby
Cut down on chocolate
Begin a course (education)
Work harder

Success, it seems, is linked directly to the resolution you decide to make. Opting for a popular one like dieting and smoking does not appear to carry the same degree of luck as picking one that you have created for yourself. It is also best to make only one resolution which should be important, heartfelt and personal to you. Off-the-cuff resolutions are, clearly, not sufficiently earnest enough to be embued with the good luck needed to last the whole year.

Beginning A New Task

Beginning a new task on New Year's Day is said to carry with it much good luck, which is why resolutions made today are supposedly more potent. This also applies to wearing a new piece of clothing - coming from the days when most people had few new clothes - but most of all it referred to starting a new piece of work which had as much to do with the fact that with the Hogmanay holiday over the bosses wanted their employees hard at work again. Nevertheless hobbies or new sports begun today are said to reflect well upon the person starting them.

Toasts

With your resolution duly announced a few more toasts are probably in order, so charge your glasses and let's hear some more. You may wish to write these toasts onto cards and hand a few to different guests so that everyone can join in. If you do give them a couple of moments to read them through.

"Slàinte mhath, slànte mhor"

pronounced phonetically (Slan-gee var, slan-gee vor)

meaning "Good health, great health".

or

"Here's to the New Year,
Here's to the past.
Here's to the laddie,
And here's to the lass.
Here's to the land,
That we hold so dear.
And here's to a' those,
That canna be here!"

or

"A guid New Year to yin and a'! And mony may ye
see,
And during a' the years to come, O happy may you
be."

The 'Wee Small Hours'

With the new year well and truly welcomed in and our good luck, almost certainly assured, guests will want to continue the party on into the 'wee small hours', or early morning. But, eventually, eyes will get heavy and feet tired from all the dancing not to mention those who are beginning to feel the effects of sampling all those interesting drinks you offered them earlier. Now, normally, any late-night party tends to just fizzle out which is a rather lacklustre way to bring to a close such a fun-filled evening. Instead, why not wind things down by getting everyone to gather around and sit down for an end-of-evening Scottish fireside tale. Turn on an armchair light and recount one of the eerie yarns in chapter five. When the story, or stories, have been told you can happily see the last of your guests away, content with the success of the evening, and retire to your own bed and some well deserved sleep.

YOUR NEW YEAR'S DAY BREAKFAST

With the excesses of the previous evening causing many of us to feel somewhat 'fragile' this morning a good healthy breakfast is just what's needed to help restore us to fine fettle and set us up for the rest of the day. A fairly light menu is therefore most suitable and fish, especially Arbroath Smokies, if prepared properly is not only good for you but a delicious first meal for the New Year. Here's our menu:

Porridge
Arbroath Smokies served with lots of hot butter.
Bacon and Potato Scones.
Morning Rolls

Porridge
Ingredients
4 ozs medium oatmeal
2 pints of water
Salt

Preparing
Boil water and add salt
Sprinkle in oatmeal while stirring
Bring back to boil whilst stirring for about five minutes
When meal swells reduce heat and allow to simmer for half an hour, stirring frequently.
Serve hot into porridge bowls adding water if required.
Sugar or salt to taste.

YOUR NEW YEAR'S DAY DINNER

In the old days what you ate for dinner on New Year's Day reflected your status in the community. For the lords it was usually a grand affair with tables bulging with the finest game and meat, a plentiful supply of the best wines and spirits not to mention exotic fruits and sweets. The lower classes could expect far less. Whether or not you ate meat on New Year's day was seen as very important and much was done to ensure this happened. Poorer families would save for months to ensure that they could afford the best Hogmanay & New Year they could, often doing without and working extra to do so. For most, having beef was essential as was the obligatory 'clootie dumpling' or pudding made by wrapping ingredients in a cloth and then boiling it. This, therefore is a traditional New Year's dinner in Scotland.

Menu
Pea Soup
Beefsteak Pie
Clootie Dumpling

Pea Soup
Ingredients
1 onion, finely chopped
Knob of butter
2 tablespoons cream
1 teaspoon sugar
2 pints chicken stock
2 lbs peas
salt
freshly ground pepper
pinch mixed herbs

Preparing
Melt butter in pot
Add in stock, and peas then the rest of the ingredients except the cream.
Simmer until peas become soft then season to taste.
Blend and sieve mixture.
Reheat prior to serving before adding cream to complete.

BeefSteak Pie
Ingredients
2 lb stewing steak
1 teaspoonful flour
Salt and pepper
½ teacupful of water or stock

Rough puff pastry

Preparing
Pre-heat oven.
Clean meat and cut into neat strips.
Mix flour and seasonings together and dip the meat into it.
Place into a pie-dish, and add water or stock.
Prepare pastry, and roll out until 1cm in thickness making pastry bigger than the pie-dish to be used.
Remove off a strip from three sides of the pastry, moisten edges of the pie-dish, and place strips around.
Moisten this edge once more and place the piece of pastry on top before pressing the edges together and trimming away any rough pieces before decorating.
Pierce a hole in the centre of the pie to allow the steam to escape.
Coat top of the pastry with water, milk or beaten egg and decorate the centre with cut-out leaves of pastry.
Place in a pre-heated hot oven till the pastry rises and browns before lowering heat and cooking for up to 2½ hours.
When done, fill up with hot water or seasoned stock and serve.

Clootie Dumpling
Ingredients
6 ozs shredded suet
6 ozs bread crumbs
6 ozs self-raising flour

6 ozs sultanas
4 ozs currants
2 teaspoons of cinnamon
2 tablespoons of black treacle
2 tablespoons of mixed spice
1 teaspoon of ground ginger
1 teaspoon of bicarbonate of soda
1½ cups of milk
½ teaspoon of ground cloves
4 ozs of brown sugar

Preparing
Dissolve treacle in the milk .
Take bowl add all ingredients and mix well until soft.
Boil a pudding cloth, wring out and sprinkle with flour.
Add mixture to cloth, close and tie off with string, allowing for expansion.
Steam at bottom of large saucepan filled with boiling water.
Boil for three hours ensuring water always covers dumpling.
Water must stay on the boil.
At end remove dumpling from water and cloth.
Dry in oven for a couple of minutes.
Serve, either hot or cold with cream or custard.

The Lull Before Another Storm?
After dinner, with a full belly, and usually a smile on your face it is time to settle quietly back in a

favourite armchair and, most probably, gently doze off for a few hours. For some, especially younger generations, there might well be plans for another party later on in the evening so it's as well to get some rest before the whirlwind of music, dancing and fun starts up again. Those who are beginning to feel the pace will probably be quite content to spend the rest of the day at a less hectic rate, perhaps starting that new hobby or piece of work they promised themselves to begin. Regardless of how the rest of New Year's Day is spent there is the warm feeling of having had a great time and the desire, in twelve months time, to do it all again!

CHAPTER FOUR

Fireside Stories To Tell...

• •

So Hogmanay's been and gone. The New Year is upon us and after a couple of hours the party will be winding down and tired guests will be thinking of making their way home. What better way to end the evening than with a traditional Scottish mystery story. These fireside tales are a good way to let everyone know the evening's come to an end and to send them off into the night with a wonderful spine-tingling feeling. You may wish to play up the storyteller's voice, adding dramatic pauses to heighten the suspense or, perhaps, ask others to join in with their own atmospheric sound effects.

Our first story is the tale of a brave hunter who found himself attacked by strange and evil magic one dark night...

The Hunter of the Hills

Many, many years ago in a Northern Scottish village there lived a brave and fearless hunter. He was an honest man who rooted out the devils and witches who terrified the locals.

One cold, dark evening as he was returning home from a day's hunting with his faithful dogs a strange and terrible storm arose. Hail lashed his face and a thick mist closed in enveloping both him and his dogs.

By luck he came across a herdsman's hut and managed to find refuge from the storm inside. No sooner had he lit a blazing fire when there came a scratching at the bolted door which he cautiously opened only to find a poor bedraggled cat huddling in the doorway against the storm. The hunter grabbed his dogs who rushed to attack the pathetic animal at which point the cat began to speak.

"I seek shelter from the storm, and warmth from your fire, brave hunter but I must confess I am a witch and ask your mercy in helping me change my evil ways. Will you invite me in?"

The hunter hesitated for a moment, for inviting a witch across the threshold is a dangerous thing to do, but took pity on the poor creature and bade it enter. The cat, however, remained where it was.

"Your dogs will tear me to shreds," it said, looking at the snarling beasts. "Take this long grey hair and bind one end to that beam and the other to their collars. Then I will enter"

The hunter did as he was told and bound one end of the grey hair to the beam but realised just in time what he was about to do and, instead, only pretended to fasten the other end to his dogs.

The cat now confidently crossed the threshold and curled up by the fire at which point it changed slowly until, finally, it was a woman who stood before him. He looked with horror at her face recognising her as a local woman from his village known for her grace and virtue.

"You, hunter...," she hissed menacingly. "It is you I have trapped in this remote hut with this tempestuous storm and now I will put an end to you!"

She flew at the hunter's throat with her strong fingers, pinning him to the floor and starting to squeeze the life from him. But his faithful dogs at once leapt at the evil witch tearing at her arms and back.

Letting out a shriek she screamed "Bind! Bind!" whereupon the magic grey hair tightened so fast upon the wooden beam that it cut it in two and would surely have killed the dogs the same way had they been bound by it.

Alas for the witch, however, the dogs were free and continued to savage her with great fury for daring to attack their master. Finally with a terrifying screech she let go her vice-like grip from the huntsman's throat and, changing before his eyes into a raven flew out of the door.

As quickly as it had begun, the storm was over and the hunter, recovering his breath, again began to make his way home.

Arriving at his village he found the people gathered outside the house of the secret witch. They told him she was out collecting fuel for her fire and had returned gravely ill. At this the hunter entered her house and stepping boldly forward flung back the sheets of the bed to reveal the horrible wounds left by his dogs. The hunter turned to the villagers and told them what had happened whereupon they seized the *evil witch and hanged her from the village tree.*

That same night, some miles away, two weary travellers on the road to the same village were horrified to see the ghostly image of a woman rushing past them into the night with two savage black dogs chasing after her like the wind. A few moments later a strange, dark rider, whose face was hidden, approached and asked if a woman had past their way. The travellers nodded, telling him of the woman and of the savage dogs chasing her, whereupon he asked if the dogs have caught her before she reached the local churchyard?

The travellers agreed that the dogs would easily have caught the woman before the church at which point the horseman gave a loud cry of delight and sped off into the night in pursuit of the woman.

Sometime later a sound like thunder on the road behind them caused the travellers to turn to see the same dark rider bearing down on them at great speed his hounds close behind. His right hand gripped the long hair of the same ghostly woman they'd seen but who now screamed and cursed as she was dragged alongside the horse, the terrible hounds leaping at her heels biting her.

The rider, woman and hounds swept past them and disappeared into the dark night but when the travellers reached the village and recounted their story all were agreed that they had seen the spirit of the witch trying desperately to reach the safety of the churchyard. But who the dark rider was they shuddered to think...

Our next story is the true tale of a desolate Scottish island where a strange and terrible mystery took place many years ago...

The Mystery Of Eilean Mor

Eilean Mor is a bleak and remote island twenty miles West of the island of Lewis in the Outer Hebrides far to the West coast of Scotland. It is one of the Flannan Islands, small, rocky specks in the cold, wild Atlantic and in 1899 a lighthouse was built to keep the passing ships away from the treacherous rocks. The powerful light on Eilean Mor was tended by three keepers who saw no one except a boat called the Hesperus which would call fortnightly with provisions, and a replacement keeper.

It was during one of the dark, bleak nights in the middle of December, 1900 that things went terribly wrong on Eilean Mor. The Hesperus had called leaving supplies and picking up keeper Joseph Moore, who stood and watched the small island disappear into the distance little realising that he would never see his companions, Thomas Marshall, James Ducat and Donald McArthur alive again.

The first sign that there was trouble came on the night of December 15th when the SS Archer nearly dashed herself on the rocks of Eilean Mor because no light was showing from the lighthouse. Realising only at the last moment the peril she was in her Captain

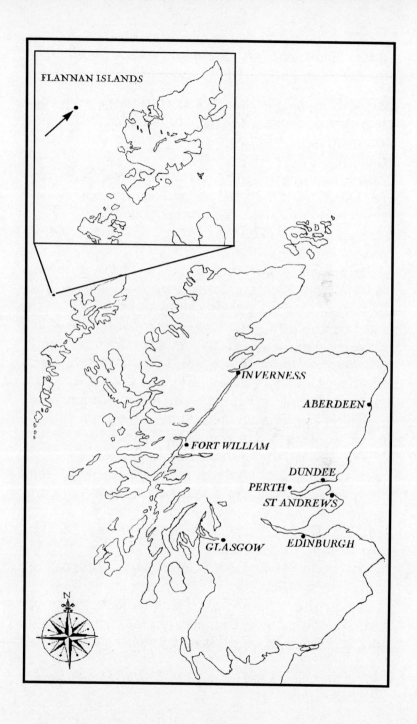

narrowly managed to steer the ship away from the jagged rocks, cursing the fools at the lighthouse who would allow the light go out in such a dangerous place.

But why was the lighthouse in darkness? The three men who tended the light were all experienced keepers who took their work very, very seriously. They were not the kind to let the light go out unless... something was gravely wrong.

Storms continued to lash Eilean Mor with each night the lighthouse remaining in darkness putting the lives of those on passing ships in peril.

It was not until nine days later when the weather eased enough for the Hesperus to reach the island that keeper Joseph Moore could be put ashore in a small boat with two other sailors in it. On reaching the jetty, Moore, at his wit's end, hurried along the small stone path up to the lighthouse when he found the gate and the main door closed.

Slowly he entered the building and shouted for the keepers. There was no reply. He made his way to the living quarters, finding them neat and tidy but with no sign of life. He tried the other rooms but, again, nothing. This only left the light tower and fearing that he may find the keepers lying dead beside the light he returned for the two sailors in the boat before going back to look.

Slowly they climbed the steps with a feeling of dread but on entering the tower found it empty except for the lamps and oil all neatly prepared and ready for use.

The men looked at each other in puzzlement and

decided to search the small island for the keepers.
This they did but found no trace of the other men.
The keepers had simply disappeared without trace.

Returning to the lighthouse Moore noticed that two
of the oilskin coats and two pairs of sea boots were
missing from the stores and also that the clock on the
mantelpiece had stopped.

He hurried to the room where Thomas Marshall's
lighthouse log was kept and looked at the last few
entries, they made grim reading...

December 12

Gale North by Northwest. Sea lashed to fury.
Stormbound. 9 p.m. Never seen such a storm. Waves
very high. Tearing at lighthouse. Everything ship-
shape. Ducat irritable.

12pm

Storm still raging. Wind steady. Stormbound.
Cannot go out. Ship passing sounding foghorn. Could
see lights of cabins. Ducat quiet. McArthur crying.

December 13

Storm continued through night. Wind shifted West
by North. Ducat quiet. McArthur praying.

12 noon

Grey daylight. Me, Ducat and McArthur prayed.

Strangely there was no entry for December 14 and only one more entry was made.

December 15

1pm

Storm ended. Sea calm. God is over all.

So what had happened to the keepers later on December 15th? Had the strange storm returned later that day, driving the men to despair? This seems unlikely as they were all veterans of the seas and had experienced many storms over the years. But why then was the old seahand McArthur crying and why had they all felt the need to pray when they were not known as religious men.

Some people suggested that one of the keepers had gone mad and killed the other two, taking their bodies and throwing them into the sea before killing himself. In this case why were none of the knives or tools missing from the stores and why were there no signs of a struggle as the keepers fought for their lives?

Others suggested that the men had been the victims of a sinister and evil force which had enveloped the island. Certainly the log shows that these experienced keepers had been terrified of something. Did they, thinking the storm was gone, find themselves caught outside, beyond the safety of the lighthouse and unable to get back in time?

Whatever the suggestion it is unlikely that we will ever know for sure what happened on that fateful dark December night on the cold, lonely island of Eilean Mor...

CONCLUSION

Next Time Hogmanay Comes Around...

So there it is – Hogmanay. A great and glorious Scottish celebration of the coming of the New Year. But no matter how much tradition surrounds this wonderful event one thing should always remain upper-most to those seeking to celebrate in true Scottish style – and that's to make sure you have a good time. True, many of the traditions almost ensure this whilst also adding a touch of colour and heritage to what should be a friendly and trouble-free party.

Hogmanay is both a chance to remember the past year as it ticks slowly out and to welcome in the new, to look forward to all the good times that lie ahead for us all. Hogmanay at its best is a good blend of friends and family, singing, dancing, eating and, of course, drinking.

The Scottish Hogmanay traditions are there for anyone and everyone to enjoy, regardless of nationality and you can be sure that if you follow them then you're probably destined to have one of the best New Year parties possible. Certainly if recent years are anything to go by the popularity of Hogmanay seems set to grow even more, drawing greater and greater numbers of people from around the world keen to welcome the New Year.

There can be no doubt that to be in Scotland at Hogmanay is a great experience with so much good cheer about it's almost impossible not to have a good time. The locals are out and about all over the country enjoying themselves and keeping alive many of the old customs like first-footing as well as the more local events we've talked about. So next time Hogmanay comes around raise a dram to yourself, your friends and your family and say

"Here's to us, fae's like us?"

GLOSSARY

ane, one

Auld, (ah-ld) old

Auld Hogmanay, January the 1st of the old calendar, now the 11th of January

auld lang syne, old long ago

Auld Reekie, Edinburgh

aye, always

bagpipes,

bairn, (bay-rn) child

bannocks, a round flat cake made of barley or oatmeal

birl, twirl

bonnet, hat

bonnie, beautiful

braes, hillsides

braw, good

brose, a mixture made by adding oatmeal to a boiling liquid

broth, a soup which is made from fish or meat stock

burn, stream

cauld, cold

ceilidh, social gathering involving dancing, music, singing and storytelling

clan, a way of life espe cially in the Scottish Highlands

clavie, a barrel filled with tar and set alight on Hogmanay to mark the occassion and drive off evil spirits

cockade, a ribbon or feather worn on a mil- itary bonnet

croft, a small plot of land, with an adjoin- ing dwelling, worked

by the inhabitants.
cromach, a hooked
walking stick

deid, dead
dinna, don't
dirk, a dagger
dram, a measure or 'tot'
of whisky

fiere, friend
first-footing, the tradi
tion of ensuring good
luck for the coming
year by following
certain customs,
namely that your first
visitor (hence 'first
foot') over your
threshold in the New
Year should be a tall,
healthy, handsome,
dark-haired man of a
generous nature
bringing with him
gifts.
fit, what

gie's, give me
gillie, Scottish hunting
guide or attendant
glen, a steep mountain
valley
gowans, daisies
guid-willie waught,
goodwill drink
guising, the act of dress
ing up and going from
house to house to
mark a special occas
sion

hae, have
haggis, traditional
Scottish meal made
from the heart, lungs,
liver of a sheep with
other ingredients espe
cially oatmeal then
boiled in the skin of
the animal's stomach
hogmanay, name given
by Scots to December
31st, or last day of the
year

ken, know
kilt, knee-length pleated
skirt, part of tradition
al Scottish Highland
garb

laird, Scottish term for
'lord'

lassie, young woman
loch, lake
lum, chimney

maun, man
mony, many
muckle, plenty
mair, more

nae, no
nicht, night

paidl'd, waded, paddled
pint-stowp, pay for
pou'd, pulled

reek, steam

sae, say
skene dhu, dirk, from
    Gaelic 'sgian dubh' or
    black knife, tucked in
    at top of sock
skirl,the sound of the
    bagpipes
Slainte mhor, (Slangee
    vharr), your health
sporran, belted fur
    pouch worn in front of
    kilt to carry small pos-
    sessions in and also as
    protection.

tae, to
tartan, a cloth, also
    distinguishs clans
toun, town
trews, trousers

wee, small
weel, well
wha's, who is

INDEX